Romantic Essentials

Hundreds of Ways to Show Your Love

Gregory Godek

Romance is the process . . . Love is the goal.

Romantic Essentials

Hundreds of Ways to Show Your Love

Gregory Godek

Casablanca Press
A Division of Sourcebooks, Inc.®
Naperville, IL

Published by Sourcebooks, Inc.

P.O. Box 4410
Naperville, IL 60567
630-961-3900
Fax: 630-961-2168

ISBN 1-57071-517-3

Printed and bound in the United States of America.
EB 10 9 8 7 6 5 4 3 2

Dedications

To the quietly brave,
the creatively intimate,
the gently strong—you are the lovers,
the peace-makers, the saviors of the world.

And, of course, to my Bride, Tracey . . .
M.H., M.S.P, M.S.K., M.P.

There is no secret when it comes to love.
There is only living it.

Other books by Gregory Godek

1001 Ways To Be Romantic

10,000 Ways To Say I Love You

The Lover's Companion

Love Coupons

*The root of our problems—**all** of our problems—
is a lack of love.*

Introduction

Hide this book. It is intended to be a "Romantic Secret Weapon"—a resource to be used when you're in a tight spot. Stash it in your glove compartment; hide it in the back of your desk drawer; toss it in the bottom of your briefcase.

This book is an extension of Gregory Godek's bestsellers *1001 Ways To Be Romantic* and *10,000 Ways To Say I Love You.* Greg's files of romantic ideas, far from being depleted by the publication of these books, have been growing exponentially. Why? Two reasons: 1) Because his creativity has been inspired by the challenge of customizing his lectures and seminars for every different audience he addresses, and 2) Because his readers keep sending him creative ideas, more resources, and stories of their crazy romantic exploits!

This book is intended to inspire you to *action.* Because romance *is* "love in action." Thus, the items in *Romantic Essentials* are practical and specific. For those of you who want more *inspiration* (or who want to inspire your *partner*), we have just published *The Lover's Companion.* It is a compilation of quotes and meditations from Greg's acclaimed Romance Seminars.

Thank you for your commitment to bringing more love into *your* life, into your *partner's* life and into this world that so desperately needs it.

1

. . . .

You don't fit *love* into your *life*—you fit your *life* into your *love*.

2

. . . .

You can't add an eighth day to the week, but you *can* add a 13th month to the year! *Really!* Harvard economist Juliet Schor reports an incredible statistic. In her book *The Overworked American*, she says that people today work more than they did 25 years ago—the equivalent, in fact, of a 13th month each year! Just *imagine* if we gave that 13th month to our lovers *instead* of our bosses!

3

. . . .

And then, of course, there's the waffle iron that makes *heart-shaped waffles!* Villaware manufactures a heart-shaped waffler available in stores and online, including www.appliances.com, or call appliances.com at 888-543-8345.

4

. . . .

Romantic Trivia: Hershey makes 33 *million* chocolate Kisses *every day!*

5

. . . .

Put a "JUST MARRIED" sign in your back windshield the next time you go for a Sunday afternoon drive . . . and enjoy the reaction from other drivers!

6

. . . .

Write "I LOVE YOU" in the dust on the coffee table.

7

. . . .

The "Rule of Romantic Reciprocity": Whenever your partner makes a romantic gesture, you have one week in which to reciprocate.

8

. . . .

Maybe your guy isn't really among the "Romantically Impaired"—perhaps he just has an unconscious aversion to the *word* "romance." Try this: Stop using the word romance altogether—and replace it with the word "fun."

9

. . . .

Just one good idea, one concept that strikes home, one insight that "feels right," is all it takes to move your relationship a quantum leap forward. You don't need this *whole* book . . . But you may need to read all of it in order to find that gem, that *"Keeper"* that will make the difference in your life.

10

. . . .

Let's be honest: Love is not *all* that you need. However . . . When you *do* have love in your life, it makes up for many things you may lack. But if you lack *love*, then no matter *what* else you have, or *how much* you have, it will never be enough.

People who are sensible about love
are incapable of it.

~ Douglas Yates

11

Create your own "Day-at-a-Time" calendar. The goal is to fill-in every day with events, information and quotes that are *unique to the two of you*. You can include your birthdays and anniversaries, but *not* the generic holidays and events like Valentine's Day or Independence Day. Include the birthdays of your favorite movie stars, singers and other people (January 29th is Oprah Winfrey's birthday; July 3rd is Tom Cruise's). Include quirky dates that have meaning for the two of you. Fill-in the rest of the dates with inspirational and funny quotes that you like.

12

When a *woman* hears the word *Romance* she thinks "Love." When a *man* hears the word *Romance* he thinks "Sex." Frankly, I don't see any problem here. This is just the way it *is*, folks. The goal is to understand your partner's point-of-view and take it into account. The goal should *not* be to convince your partner that your view is the "correct" one. We need love; we need sex. Romance is a bridge that connects the two.

13

A *must* for your Romantic Music Library:

☆ *Sunny,* by rising superstar singer and inspirational speaker Willie Jolley. This just-released recording is a collection of Willie's jazz-style interpretations of classics such as "Ain't No Sunshine" and "My Funny Valentine."

Just $12.99, from InspirTainment Plus. Write to them at 5711 13th Street NW, Suite 100, Washington, D.C. 20011. Or call 202-723-8863.

P.S.—If you like Gospel music, ask for the album *Blessed Assurance.*
P.P.S.—If you'd like to jazz up your Christmas, ask for Willie Jolley's album *We Wish You a Merry Jolley Christmas.*

14

Tracey recently gave me a great gift that's been keeping us entertained for *months.* It's a little box full of *words . . .* 400 words on little magnets. They're on our refrigerator, and we create notes and poems for each other nearly every day. Available at bookstores and specialty stores, or check out their website at www.magneticpoetry.com.

15

Which singer, in which song, has sung the words "I love you" the best? Who sings these quintessential words with the most *feeling*, the most *passion?* Perhaps it's Olivia Newton John singing *I Honestly Love You.* My vote goes to Justin Hayward, in a verse toward the end of *Nights In White Satin*, on the Moody Blues' CD *Days of Future Passed.*

16

Replace your old pajamas with silk boxer shorts.

17

A sudden insight from a Romance Class participant: "Being romantic is actually being *selfish!* From the sound of it, if I'm more romantic, *I'm* the one who's going to gain lots of benefits: More frequent sex, more *passionate* sex, more cooperation, less nagging, more surprises! Where do I sign up?!"

18

. . . .

While the two of you are out grocery shopping or running errands, have a friend deliver and set out a gourmet dinner, complete with your best china, candles, and soft music. (Don't forget to return the favor.)

19

. . . .

The 10 most important words in any loving relationship:

- ✳ Trust
- ✳ Intimacy
- ✳ Communication
- ✳ Commitment
- ✳ Love
- ✳ Friendship
- ✳ Patience
- ✳ Humor
- ✳ Flexibility
- ✳ Forgiveness

20

From an informal survey, asking women what phrases they consider most romantic:

- ✦ "I love you."
- ✦ "Will you marry me?"
- ✦ "Dinner at the Ritz."

21

From an informal survey, asking men what phrases they consider most romantic:

- ✧ "You mean the world to me."
- ✧ "Dinner's ready!"
- ✧ "Happy birthday! I got you season tickets to the Red Sox!"

22

A cruise ship tip: Book your berth *early* and request a *double bed*—they're very scarce on most cruise ships!

23-25

· ·

If your spiritual journey impels you to visit sacred spaces and places of spiritual significance, you may want to consider vacationing in these spots:

- ☆ **Sedona, Arizona:** Many people sense "energy vortices" in this area.
- ☆ **Stonehenge, England:** The mysterious neolithic astronomical calendar created from a circle of stone monoliths.
- ☆ **Coral Castle, in Homestead, Florida:** A home built as a monument to a lost love, Coral Castle is an eerie fantasy created from rock and fashioned with primitive hand tools by an immigrant between 1920 and 1940. Described as one of the wonders of the modern world, no one knows how the huge boulders were moved to the site from the surrounding countryside.

For more info, or to book a journey, call VIP Travel at 800-9999-VIP.

- ☆ The travel specialists at VIP can also recommend romantic locations, create custom vacations, and give you the best value for your budget!

26

. . . .

Don't buy him a dozen roses for Valentine's Day. —*Instead*, buy him a dozen new *wrenches* . . . tie them with a red ribbon . . . and present them in a fancy vase. {Thanks to Michelle R., Schaumburg, Illinois}

27

. . . .

Americans celebrate Independence Day on July 4th . . . *I* think we need to celebrate an "**Inter**dependence Day"—to acknowledge and celebrate the fact that relationships work best when we are neither dependent nor independent. How about celebrating this new holiday on January 4th—six months after Independence Day?

28

. . . .

Attach a note to your partner's calculator: ***"You can count on me."***

29

On August 3, 1964, during a walk on the beach with his wife, Howard W. drew a heart in the sand, and inscribed his initials entwined with his wife's initials. The next day when they returned to the same spot (near their home on Cape Cod, Massachusetts), the surf had washed his handiwork away. Undaunted, he drew the same message *again*, saying, "Love needs to be renewed every day, too." *Howard has drawn the same heart and initials in the sand every day for the past 30 years!*

30

I have an authentic boomerang in my office, from a trip to Australia last year. Recently, before leaving for a week-long conference, I left it on Tracey's nightstand with a note: *"I'll **always return** to you."*

31

Attach a note to your partner's wristwatch: *"It's **time for love.**"*

32

. . . .

Attach a note to the TV remote control: *"Turn **me** on instead!"*

33

. . . .

Make your own greeting cards. Store-bought cards are fine—I have a drawer full of them…but homemade cards are extra-special. You don't have to be artistic, just heartfelt. (Remember, she's with you not because you're Picasso, but because you're *you*.)

It is not a lack of love,
but a lack of friendship that makes
unhappy marriages.

~ Friedrich Nietzsche

34

For those of you whose romantic hero is James Bond . . . here is the official recipe for his dry martini:

*Three measures of Gordon's,
one of vodka, half a measure of Kina Lillet.
Shake well until ice-cold, then add a large,
thin slice of lemon peel.*

35

For *some* people, dining out is about ambiance and relaxing. For *others,* it's about discovery and adventure. Matthew and Angelina, hosts of "Love Life Radio" in Hawaii, have perfected what they call "Restaurant-Hopping." In one evening they will visit seven different restaurants, ordering one course in each establishment: 1) Drinks, 2) appetizer, 3) soup, 4) salad, 5) main course, 6) dessert, 7) after-dinner drinks.

36

Believe.

37

Celebrate.

38

Connect.

39

Feel.

40

. . . .

Oprah once surprised her beau, Stedman Graham, with a new golf bag—filled to the *brim* with golf balls! Why? Just because he happened to mention that he'd spied a great new bag. Question: Was it the gift *itself*, the *surprise*, or the *sentiment* that made this gift so special? Answer: *All of the above!*

41-44

. . . .

As far as I'm concerned, *anything* that helps you understand yourself and your partner better is A Good Thing. Try dabbling in some "alternative" techniques:

- ☆ Have your Tarot Cards read.
- ☆ Dabble in Numerology.
- ☆ Discover Enneagrams.
- ☆ Have your astrological charts read.

45

Consider visiting Bologna, Italy, where they host an annual "Erotica Festival"! Call your local travel agent for details! [We at Casablanca Press accept *absolutely no responsibility* for what you may witness or experience!]

46

Get up extra-early on a weekday and go out for breakfast with your lover. It's a great way to start the day in a totally different way.

47

A homemade greeting card from one spry senior citizen to his wife:

"I've fallen in love and I can't get up!"

48

"Don't worry—be happy!" Worrying suffocates all romantic impulses. It smothers your loving feelings. It also shuts-down the *logical* portion of your brain that helps you plan and implement romantic activities. Read the classic *How To Stop Worrying And Start Living*, by Dale Carnegie.

49

How about an elegant, *custom-made* greeting card for your honey? Your favorite verse or quote—or an original romantic line—will be rendered in calligraphy, and then decorated with a one-of-a-kind hand-painted flower. Includes a matching envelope with address in calligraphy. Around $50—and well worth it! Call 508-234-6843, or fax 508-234-5446, or send info to Pendragon Ink, 27 Prospect Street, Whitinsville, Massachusetts 01588. Turn-around: Less than one week! They'll mail it or overnight it to you!

50

. . . .

A memo to Ford Motor Company:

On behalf of romantics everywhere, I respectfully submit to you that your emphasis on aerodynamics and safety, while laudable, has been accomplished, in part, by the sacrifice of comfort and convenience of those who utilize automobiles for romantic activities. Must I spell it out? You have sacrificed copulatory comfort for fuel economy—a poor trade, we think!

It appears that automobile makers have lost touch with Real People, and with the uses for which we purchase your products. In the Good Old Days, you may recall, motor carriages were roomy, to accommodate the elaborate costumery of the day. Couples were able to stand upright while dressing or undressing—having, of course, drawn the curtains that were provided as standard equipment then.

We, the romantics of America, call for the return of the roomy backseat!

Respectfully and romantically submitted,

Gregory Godek

51

. . . .

A memo to Victoria's Secret:

On behalf of romantic men everywhere (many of whom are your customers), I am writing to point out an oversight in the design of some of your lovely products. You know those "snaps" in the crotch of some of your items? Well, they are so *small* that many men have a difficult time manipulating them. It is not that we are uncoordinated, or—heavens!—*insensitive* to the needs of our lovers. It is, rather, that our fingers are larger, and therefore, less adept at accomplishing delicate maneuvers in, shall we say, delicate areas.

For those who might suggest that we let the ladies snap and unsnap their *own* snaps, we would reply that many of us feel that it is the gentlemanly thing to do, to handle (no pun intended) such responsibilities. And, *practically* speaking, very often, our partner's hands are otherwise occupied.

The solution, we feel, is simple. Replace the offending *little* snaps with *larger* snaps. Although we have not undertaken a cost analysis of such a change in your manufacturing operation, several of us are accountants, and we estimate the added cost of the larger snaps to be minimal. Also, we believe, if you were to conduct a cost-benefit analysis, you would find the benefit to your customers to be substantial (customers being defined both as the men/purchasers and the women/wearers).

Thank you for your time and attention to this delicate but important matter.

Respectfully and romantically submitted,

Gregory Godek

52

· ·

A memo to Trojan:

On behalf of responsible lovers everywhere, I would like to offer a suggestion to your Packaging Design Department that might increase the use of your fine product. As you well know, the clinical nature of your fine product is often a turn-off (no pun intended) to its users. Opening those little sealed foil packages is like popping open an Alka-Seltzer. While Alka-Seltzer, also, is a fine product, the users of *your* product do not want to be thinking about upset stomachs as they are preparing for the upcoming activity.

What is needed, we believe, is a way to make your product more "fun." A way, if you will, to make its users actually *look forward* to using the product! How, you ask, could this be accomplished? We believe a lesson could be learned from another fine product, Salada Tea Bags. Here is our idea: You, too, could include an inspirational thought or quotable quote with each of your products. For example: "Sex alleviates tension. Love causes it." ~ Woody Allen. "I'd rather hit than have sex." ~ Reggie Jackson. "When I'm good I'm very good, but when I'm bad I'm better." ~ Mae West.

Respectfully and romantically submitted,

Gregory Godek

P.S. *Another* approach has been inspired by our Chinese friends. How about the "Fortune Cookie Condom"? Mysterious and entertaining fortunes could be coupled (again, no pun intended) with each of your products. "You are about to meet a mysterious, horizontal stranger." "Please beware, and enter with care." Many other fortunes, are, of course, possible.

53

· · · · · · · · · · · · ·

A memo to United Airlines:

As a frequent flyer and longtime romantic, I have a delicate, yet serious issue to bring up with you: The Mile High Club. It has come to my attention, especially from folks over six feet tall, and from representatives of the NBA, that the cramped size of the restrooms on your airplanes makes it difficult—if not completely *impossible*—for many people to make love in them.

We have taken the liberty to measure the restrooms and adjacent seats in one of your 747s. I think you will be pleased to know that the Restroom Expansion Project would only require the removal of *two* seats! We estimate that United Airlines will not suffer *any* financial loss due to the loss of these seats, as most flights are not fully-booked anyway. Also, we estimate that the re-design costs, plus the addition of strategically-placed "bumper pads" would cost less than $1,000 per plane. This nominal cost would be made up in increased consumer demand for these special flights.

From a marketing point-of-view, this innovation could propel you into the forefront of the airline industry. Some time in the future, *all* planes will include such amenities—but for now, this consumer benefit could give you a significant competitive advantage.

I understand your reticence to deal with this issue, being of such a delicate and intimate nature. Yet I urge you to be *bold!* This innovation could be the change that invigorates the entire airline industry. Just think, you could lead the way, post increased profits, and earn the undying gratitude of romantics everywhere.

Respectfully and romantically submitted,

Gregory Godek

54

. . . .

Are romantics *born* or *made?* Are some guys genetically inclined to be romantic, while others are genetically destined to be, say, *accountants?* Well, I'm here to tell you with certainty that romantics are *made.* How do I know this? Because my brother Gary, a mere four years younger than I—and raised by the same parents in the same loving environment that I grew up in—*does not have a romantic bone in his body.* If romance were in the genes, then he'd be romantic, too. Thus, romance is not an inborn ability; it is a *teachable talent.* (This is Good News to accountant's spouses everywhere.)

55

. . . .

News for men: Women like a gentleman.

56

. . . .

News for women: Men like women with long hair.

57

. . . .

News for men: Women want you to share your feelings. (Sharing feelings *doesn't* make you a wimp. —It's being insecure and weak-willed that's wimpy.)

58

. . . .

News for women: Men *like* women with **curves.** (Most of us do *not* lust after the anorexic models in your magazines.)

59

. . . .

News for men: When a woman says she wants more romance, she doesn't mean that she wants more *gifts.* —She wants more *thoughtfulness.*

60

. . . .

For the sports lover in your life: Autographed baseballs!

Get an authentic hand-signed ball autographed by his favorite player, or get the "500 Home Run Club Baseball," signed by ten players who have hit five hundred home runs or more. Includes Henry Aaron, Willie Mays, Frank Robinson, Reggie Jackson, and Mickey Mantle.

Visit the Hammacher Schlemmer website at www.hammacher.com.

61

. . . .

+ And then there was the couple who got married via teleconferencing.
+ And then there was the couple who exchanged vows while skydiving.
+ And then there was the couple who got married on Halloween night . . . at midnight . . . dressed as Dracula and the Bride of Frankenstein . . . with the guests in costume . . . and the waiters dressed as zombies.

62

Don't take *sex* so seriously! A light attitude goes along with a light touch. Good natured humor will get you through most any sexual glitch!

63

Have a pair of wine goblets etched with your names (or initials).

64

Building on the above idea . . . Secretly deliver your special wine goblets ahead of time to the restaurant where you'll be dining tonight! {Thanks to Butch/Jerry Engel, our favorite Marathon Man.}

65

Stuff that works:

- 🍃 Live your life as if you were an exclamation point!
- 🍃 When two people always agree, one of them is no longer necessary.
- 🍃 There is no way to happiness. Happiness is the way.

From a great little book, *Stuff That Works Every Single Day*, by Larry Winget. Available in bookstores or online.

66

Warning for habitual Internet surfers: "Virtual Love" is way different from the Real Thing. If there's no face time, you don't have a *real* relationship. The Net is cool for intros and fun, but until Bill Gates perfects a Star Trek-like holodeck where we can meet in true Virtual Reality, the Net remains a nice place to visit, but not a place to live.

67

. . . .

One couple in the Romance Class shared with us a "Relationship Prayer" they'd written on their 10th anniversary. They now recite it every night.

> Lord, help us remember that our love for each other
> Reflects Your love for us.
> May we empower one another to fulfill
> Our Purpose in life.
> May our love be an example for our children
> And a model for all.
> May our experience as a couple give us a preview of
> The Oneness we will experience some day.
> Help us to see that everything is either Love
> Or a call for Love.
> Help us to celebrate our similarities
> And honor our differences.
> Help us to accept our limitations
> And utilize our talents.
> Thank you for this opportunity, this life,
> And for my loving partner.
> Amen.

68

. . . .

File under "Welcome to the Real World" . . . a report from the *Wall Street Journal:* "A growing body of research suggests many male professionals wish for a better balance between work and family and get frustrated when employers don't recognize that desire . . . Based on a summary of recent research, Dr. Kimmel says few men fit stereotypes of the distant father and work-obsessed breadwinner."

69

. . . .

What's her all-time favorite meal? Learn to make it! Get help from friends, neighbors, or relatives—whatever it takes.

70

When's the last time you watched cloud formations? Take your lover for a walk in a field. Find an unobstructed view. Flop down on a hilltop. What do you see in the clouds? What do you imagine? (What *else* might you two be able to do together in the middle of a field??)

71

Want to stay in touch? Buy her a cellular phone as a surprise. Put a ribbon on it, hide it in a closet, and call her from another room in the house. {Thanks to Kathy Torpey-Garganta!}

72

Unique, classy, romantic . . . cards, wrappings, ideas, gifts 'n stuff—from the *Victorian Papers Catalog:* 800-800-6647.

73

. . . .

Have you ever noticed that some people are able to survive—and succeed!—despite the most difficult circumstances, while others who have every advantage seem determined to self-destruct? No one knows exactly why this is, but Harvard professor of psychiatry George Vaillant has some clues. The *Boston Globe* reports that he has identified "two key factors that allow certain people to 'spin straw into gold': 1) the ability to handle life's woes with humor, empathy, and a certain kind of creative resourcefulness; and 2) the kismet of finding supportive spouses who care deeply about them and are able to make up for deprivations suffered as children."

74

. . . .

Karma is "action."
Romance is "love in action."
Thus, romance *is* karma!
(A little lesson in romantic Buddhism.)

Conflict and love:
do they go together? Absolutely!
Do most couples realize that conflict is an
opportunity to help their love grow? No, they do not.
Your conflict can be loving and productive,
and both of you can win.

~ Larry Losoncy

75

Cynics say that "Familiarity breeds contempt." Romantics know that it's *poor relationships* that breed contempt, not the familiarity. And now we have studies that confirm our belief. Several studies indicate that sexual frequency and satisfaction both climb when the children leave home and couples spend more time together. The *Janus Report on Sexual Behavior* reports that men's sexual frequency is highest in their 50s (!)—and that women over 65 with partners are as sexually active as women in their late 20s (!!)

76

Speaking of sexual myths . . . It is *not* true that men's sexual capacity declines after a peak in the teenage years. [*Whew!*] Speed of orgasm and short-term frequency do decline somewhat, but interest and ability to climax on a regular basis are not affected.

77

And another sexual myth . . . It is *not* true that women lose interest in sex after menopause. In fact, most surveys of sexual behavior find an upswing in sexual frequency for women over 65 who have partners. Go for it!

78

Different stages of relationships have different goals. Relationships are "about" different things at different times. What stage are you in? What are your wants and needs? How do they compare with your partner's?

What do you need *right now?* . . .

✧ Connection	✧ Appreciation	✧ Understanding
✧ Comfort	✧ Security	✧ Friendship
✧ Being known	✧ Enchantment	✧ Excitement
✧ Intimacy	✧ Sex	✧ Passion

79

Half a tattoo is better than one [I *think* . . !] Christine and Matthew M., of Topeka, Kansas, each got half a heart tattooed on their forearms. When they press their arms together, they form one complete heart!

80

Experiment with some alleged aphrodisiacs. Couldn't hurt. Might help!

- ☆ **Oysters:** Most potent when eaten plain.
- ☆ **Caviar:** The largest type, Beluga, is James Bond's favorite.
- ☆ **Nutmeg:** Has a reputation in the Far East as an aphrodisiac.
- ☆ **Saffron:** Expensive—because it takes 100,000 saffron crocus flowers to produce one pound of saffron!
- ☆ **Ginger:** An aphrodisiac used in China for 3,000 years.
- ☆ **Fenugreek:** Contains diosgenin, used in the synthesis of sex hormones. Sold in Chinese health food shops as a restorative.

81

Okay guys, if nothing *else* has motivated you to eat a healthier diet and reduce your fat intake, perhaps *this* will do it: *Fatty diets have been linked with impotence.* "Just as fat in the bloodstream can build blockages in the arteries of the heart, so can it build blockages in the arteries of the penis, interfering with blood circulation. Then a kind of heart attack of the penis may occur, and a man has difficulty having an erection," reports the *Boston Herald.* Need I say more?!

82

"Emotions are contagious," according to psychoanalyst Carl Jung. Recent studies are proving him correct. It seems that some people have a natural ability to transmit moods, while others are more susceptible to "catching" moods from others. The transmission of moods is an instantaneous and unconscious process.

Are you a *sender* or a *receiver?* How about your partner? Pay close attention to your moods for the next week to see if you detect any recurring patterns.

83-85

. . . .

Some books *about* men, *for* men, *by* men:

- ☆ *Myths of Masculinity*, by William Doty
- ☆ *The End of Manhood: A Book for Men of Conscience*, by John Stoltenberg
- ☆ *Boys Will Be Men: Masculinity in Troubled Times*, by Richard Hawley

86-88

. . . .

More books about men, for men, by men:

- ☞ *The Lover Within: Accessing the Lover in the Male Psyche*, by Robert Moore
- ☞ *Sexual Peace: Beyond the Dominator Virus*, by Michael Sky
- ☞ *American Manhood: Transformations in Masculinity From the Revolution to the Modern Era*, by E. Anthony Rotundo

89-91

. . . .

Some books *about* women, *for* women, *by* women:

- ➻ *Moving Beyond Words*, by Gloria Steinem
- ➻ *Reinventing Love: Six Women Talk About Love, Lust, Sex, and Romance*, by Laurie Abraham, et al.
- ➻ *A Woman's Worth*, by Marianne Williamson

92-94

. . . .

Some books *about* couples, *for* couples:

- ❦ *The Language of Love: A Powerful Way to Maximize Insight, Intimacy, and Understanding*, by Gary Smalley & John Trent
- ❦ *Perfect Husbands (& Other Fairy Tales): Demystifying Marriage, Men, and Romance*, by Regina Barreca
- ❦ *Who's On Top, Who's On Bottom: How Couples Can Learn to Share Power*, by Robert Schwebel

95-97

. . . .

Some books about love, for *singles:*

- 🍂 *Sex, Love, or Infatuation: How Can I Really Know?* by Ray Short
- 🍂 *Finding the Love of Your Life: Ten Principles for Choosing the Right Marriage Partner*, by Neil Clark Warren
- 🍂 *All the Good Ones Aren't Taken*, by Jeffrey Ullman (founder of Great Expectations video dating service)

98-100

. . . .

Some books specifically about marriage:

- ♥ *Growing A Healthy Marriage*, edited by Mike Yorkey
- ♥ *Can This Marriage Be Saved?* by Margery Rosen
- ♥ *In The Mood*, by Doreen Virtue

101-103

. . . .

Some books on love and such stuff:

* ❊ *Heart Over Heels*, by Bob Mandel
* ❊ *Too Close For Comfort: Exploring the Risks of Intimacy*, by Geraldine Piorkowski
* ❊ *1001 Ways To Be Romantic*, by some guy named Godek

104-106

. . . .

Some books on erotica and sex:

* ❤ *The Erotic in Literature: A Historical Survey of Pornography as Delightful as It Is Indiscreet*, by David Loth
* ❤ *Women Who Love Sex*, by Gina Ogden
* ❤ *203 Ways to Drive a Man Wild in Bed*, by Olivia St. Claire

107

Speaking of *books*, I've heard *many* tales about singles finding dates in bookstores. It's *easy* to start a conversation with a stranger who's holding a book by your favorite author!

108

Are you and your lover *soulmates?* What *is* a soulmate? Do you *believe* in the concept? Does your *partner?*

109-111

Books on soulmates:

- ☞ *Soul Mates: Honoring the Mysteries of Love and Relationship*, by Thomas Moore
- ☞ *Finding Your Soul Mate*, by "Michael"
- ☞ *A Bridge Across Forever*, by Richard Bach

112

"How to Keep A Marriage Together for at Least 25 Years." Some relationship tips from the lives of Linda and Paul: Believe in old-fashioned values, like love and family. Take your wife and kids with you on extended business trips. Wed your true love. {Linda and Paul *McCartney*}

113

"How to Wreck Your Lives in Just a Few Short Years." Some relationship tips from the lives of Charlie and Diane: Focus on the superficial. Put your job before your marriage. Cheat on your spouse. {Prince Charles and Di}

114

Little or no learning takes place where there's fear or guilt present. You can't *threaten* your partner into changing. You can't *shame* your partner into being romantic. You've got to use *positive, supportive* methods of communication.

115

. . . .

I can't speak from *experience* on this one, but I can at least let you *know* about . . . *clothing-optional cruises.* Nudist beaches are *easy* to find, but nudist Caribbean cruises are rare. For more info, call the Bare Necessities Tour & Travel Company at 800-743-0405, or 512-499-0405. [No, I *don't* make-up this stuff. I just report it!]

116

. . . .

"Shared secrets" can be a source of intimacy. Your pet names for one another. Private hideaways. Afternoon rendezvous. Code phrases. Note: Don't share your secrets with anyone else—not even your closest friend. The specialness will evaporate. {Thanks to Beth Wolfensberger at *The Boston Phoenix*.}

117

. . . .

"If a cellular telephone rings deep in the forest, and you are there to hear it, are you *really* on vacation?" {Andrew M., from Boston}

118

One day in the Romance Class, Nancy G. told us that she and her husband have instituted a "Play Day" once a month. The class quickly leaped on the idea and expanded upon it. So we now have couples celebrating their own "Music Days," "Food Days," and, of course, "Sex Days."

119

For the child in your lover: Mickey Mouse watches, Donald Duck tie tacks, limited edition cartoon cels, character figurines, shirts, jackets and more—available from the *Disney Catalog*. Call 800-237-5751, or write Post Office Box 29144, Shawnee Mission, Kansas 66201.

120

Go shopping for great/funny/loving birthday cards that "fit" your lover perfectly. Cross-off the word "birthday," and send the cards on *any* day! {T.E.G.}

121

Sally H., an unabashed reader from Chicago, writes: "A man's attention to *foreplay* indicates his knowledge of *sex*. But his attention to *afterplay* indicates his knowledge of *love*."

122

Romantics have a heightened awareness and appreciation of *time*. Here are some fascinating thoughts from a gem of a book, *Einstein's Dreams*, by Alan Lightman: "For the children, time moves too slowly already. They rush from moment to moment, anxious for birthdays and new years, barely able to wait for the rest of their lives . . . The elderly desperately wish to halt time . . . For the elderly, time darts by much too quickly. They yearn to capture a single minute at the breakfast table drinking tea, or a moment when a grandchild is stuck getting out of her costume, or an afternoon when the winter sun reflects off the snow and floods the music room with light."

123

. . . .

The latest studies indicate that the factors that best predict divorce are criticism, contempt, defensiveness and withdrawal. Psychologist Howard Markham says, "It's not the amount of empathy or understanding in a relationship that predicts who is going to make it and who is going to divorce. It's the zingers or negative behaviors that are far more predictive over time. As we say, one zinger erases 20 positive acts of kindness."

124

. . . .

Split a banana split. Dance the night away. Go singing in the rain.

125

. . . .

From my favorite newspaper columnist, Beverly Beckham: "There are two things you give your children. One is roots, the other is wings." Romantics, too, need roots and wings. Roots of security and commitment; wings of love and passion.

126

Creative Christmas tree ornaments:

- ❦ Music CDs (they reflect colored lights like crazy!)
- ❦ Season tickets (hung individually all over the tree!)
- ❦ Car keys (to a new car parked in the driveway with a red bow around it!)

127

Keeping perspective: "What's really important in my life?" When do we ask—much less *answer*—this question? Often, it's not until someone we love dies, or when we, ourselves, are near death, or are facing some life-altering catastrophe. Why can't/don't/won't we do it sooner and voluntarily? Many things cause us to lose perspective: Work, striving for good grades, family, the news, etc. What can we do to regain perspective?

Some ideas: 1) Have well-defined "Life Goals," 2) Identify "Personal Goals," "Couple Goals," "Family Goals," and "Career Goals," 3) Discuss them with your partner regularly, and re-evaluate them yearly.

128

For those who believe that money—as *well* as love—makes the world go 'round: Give her ten $10 bills on your tenth anniversary. Give him twenty $20 bills on his twentieth birthday. Give her fifty $50 bills . . . you get the idea.

129

"How do you get a friendship to catch fire?" Hmmm . . . You add kindling (creative ideas); you gently fan the flames (stay with it), and have patience. But—you've got to be smart enough to know if you're starting with wet wood to begin with! Some relationships will *never* catch fire.

130

Romance is a *bridge*. It's about reaching out and connecting with another person. It's about meeting in the middle.

Love is not an emptiness longing to be filled—
it is a fullness pressing to be released.

~ J. Kennedy Shultz

131

You'll find some very specific strategies for working-out arguments and other relationship difficulties in *We Can Work It Out*, by Howard Markman and Clifford Notarius. Also, *When Love Dies: The Process of Marital Disaffection*, by Karen Kayser.

132

For single women only: If there's a shortage of "good men" where you live, here's *Cosmo's* "DESIRABLE-CITIES LIST." ("Each city recommended here has a higher percentage of men eighteen to thirty-four than of women in the same age-group. That means there's less competition from other women and, the experts say, a male mind-set of scarcity, which makes a man more appreciative of the woman he's with.")

- ✦ Anchorage, Alaska
- ✦ Las Vegas, Nevada
- ✦ Norfolk, Virginia
- ✦ Phoenix/Scottsdale, Arizona
- ✦ Billings, Montana
- ✦ Denver, Colorado
- ✦ San Diego, California

133

. . . .

From an interior designer who attended a Romance Class: "Here's a subtle bedroom tip: If you've got blonde hair, use *dark* sheets and pillowcases. Your hair will be highlighted. By enhancing one of your best features, you'll be more alluring to your partner!" Couldn't hurt. Might help!

134

. . . .

For *some* people, being romantic involves major changes in their thinking and lifestyle. Be *patient* with them! Perhaps they and we could learn some lessons from those who study how people change habits: "The early phases of change demand self-understanding; the later ones demand new conduct . . . In the early stages, people must grapple with why they need their habits and how they defend them; launching into action prematurely would undermine necessary self-understanding." {Madeline Drexler in the *Boston Globe*}

135

Maybe it's just *me*, but I do believe that, in general, it's easier to buy gifts for *men* than for *women*. We men tend to be more *fanatical* about our hobbies, and *anything* you get that relates to them will be appreciated: Golf balls, fishing rods, software, sailing gear, car parts, power tools.

136

Women, in general, are harder to buy gifts for. Their interests tend to be more diverse; they're not as fanatical as guys, and they don't want practical gifts. [I *know* these are generalizations. So *please* don't write and lecture me! —If you want to write, send me some romantic ideas, and I'll include you in the next book!]

137

Rent a motorcycle for a weekend. Tour the countryside. Straddle the bike and your partner; feel the throbbing, vibration of the powerful . . . [—*You take it from here!*]

138

. . . .

An observation/theory put forth for your consideration: *Men get more conservative as they get older; women get more rebellious.* Hmmm. Seems to ring true to me. This and more, in Gloria Steinem's new book, *Moving Beyond Words.*

139

. . . .

Always kiss each other upon departing.

140

. . . .

No time to read? Then get this audio cassette tape, and learn something during your commute to work: "Men and Women: Talking Together." It brings together two leaders in the world of male-female communication: Deborah Tannen (author of the bestseller *You Just Don't Understand*) and Robert Bly (author of the bestseller *Iron John*). Together they examine how "gender dialect" works.

141

. . . .

I talk a lot about *giving* in my books and classes, but *receiving* is just as important. You must learn to accept gifts graciously, and express gratitude genuinely. And, you must learn the skill of tactfully telling your partner when you don't like a particular gift!

142

. . . .

- ■ "Men are like children. They need to be the center of attention."
- ■ "Relationships matter more to us [women] than they do to men."
- ■ "A man wants a woman who will feed his ego. Men need this desperately."

Do you believe these generalizations? Is your husband a stereotype? Are you into feeling superior—or creating a loving relationship?

The quotes above are from from Ms. Sydney Biddle Barrows. Her qualifications are six years of managing the Cachet escort/prostitution service. Ms. Barrows, popularly known as the "Mayflower Madam," 41, has never been married. [Don't confuse the knowledge of sex with the understanding of love.]

143

Practice "Leap Year Romance." When February 29th rolls around, take the day off work and declare it your own personal "Romance Day." (Hey, why should your *employer* get that extra day??—especially if you're on salary! Give the gift of time—24 hours worth—to your lover!)

144-145

➤ Learn to sing your favorite lovesong together—in *harmony!*

➤ Learn to sing a romantic duet!

- ♥ *Almost Paradise*, by Reno & Wilson
- ♥ *Nothing's Gonna Stop Us Now*, by Starship
- ♥ *Always*, by Atlantic Starr
- ♥ *Islands in the Stream*, by Parton & Rogers
- ♥ *Somewhere Out There*, by Ronstadt & Ingram
- ♥ *Time of My Life*, from Dirty Dancing

146

Some "quiet-thoughtful" methods for generating creative romantic ideas:
1) Meditate, 2) Solitude, 3) Relax with classical or instrumental music. Let the ideas just bubble-up on their own.

147

Some *active* methods for generating creative romantic ideas: 1) Keep a journal, 2) Read some books, 3) Hold a "Romantic Idea Brainstorming Party" with some friends.

148

Some *more* strategies for generating creative romantic ideas: 1) Go window shopping, 2) Keep a pad handy to jot-down ideas when they pop into your head (in the car, on the bedstand), and 3) Take some adult education classes.

149

Yes, there are many sources of happiness, but studies indicate that for most people, 85% of our happiness comes from our intimate relationship. So why do most of us spend only 2% of our time working on it??

150-156

+ Yes, love *can* be a struggle—but it's *not* a battle.

+ True, "Love makes the world go 'round"—but nobody really *believes* it.

+ They say "Money can't buy you love"—but it *can* buy a dozen red roses.

+ "It takes two to Tango"—but you can't both lead at the same time.

+ Whoever said "All's fair in love and war" probably cheated at both.

+ You may have a "Marriage made in heaven"—but you have to live it on earth!

+ True, "Love is blind"—but it's not *stupid!!*

157-163

For your Romantic/Erotic Library . . . "Erotica for women":

- ❖ *Slow Hand: Women Writing Erotica*, edited by Michele Slung
- ❖ *Fever: Sensual Stories by Women Writers*, another collection from M. Slung
- ❖ *Women On Top*, by Nancy Friday
- ❖ *Good Sex: Stories From Real People*, by Julia Hutton
- ❖ *Gates of Paradise*, by Alberto Manguel
- ❖ *Erotica*, edited by Margaret Reynolds
- ❖ *The Doctor Is In*, by Charlotte Rose

164

John Mangos, host of the "At Home" TV show in Sydney, Australia, related a story to me about his courting of a lovely Aussie lass. After six exasperating weeks of pursuit, with little response from her, he sent her a tennis racquet with a note attached: *"The ball is in your court."* It worked!

165

. . . .

"The problem in the Singles World is that the women are looking for decent men, while the men are looking for indecent women!" {Susan M., in a recent Romance Class}

166

. . . .

More gift catalogs:

- ❖ *The Smithsonian:* 800-322-0344
- ❖ *Playboy:* 800-423-9494
- ❖ *Neiman Marcus:* 800-825-8000
- ❖ *Worldwide Games:* 800-888-0987
- ❖ *Sporty's:* 800-543-8633
- ❖ *Sundance:* 800-422-2770
- ❖ *The Nature Company:* 800-227-1114
- ❖ *Rick's Movie Graphics:* 800-252-0425

It is only with the heart that one can see rightly;
what is essential is invisible to the eye.

- Antoine de Saint-Exupery

167-169

. . . .

Some couples have morning rituals:

- ↦ They spend ten minutes talking in bed before rising.
- ↦ They read an affirmation aloud to one another.
- ↦ The make a point of kissing before parting.

170-171

. . . .

Gifts for the lovable knucklehead in your life:

- ❧ The *Three Stooges* wristwatch. *"Nyuk, nyuk, nyuk!"*—only $39.95.
- ❧ The Larry, Moe and Curly necktie. *"What are you, a wisenheimer?!"*—just $36.

From the *Wireless Catalog*. Call 800-669-9999.

172

One couple is "coasting" through their relationship. And quite happily, I might add. Note: Their definition of "coasting," however, is to travel and vacation along *all* of the ocean coasts in the United States! So far, they've coasted from Calais, Maine to Corpus Christi, Texas. It's taken them seven years, and they plan to coast up the West Coast of the U.S. in the next five years. (*Then*, they're going to take-on South America!)

173

Tell her you love her every day. Every day. Every day. Every day. Every day. Every day.

174

The "Geese Mate For Life" pin. A classy, meaningful gift. Two geese are majestically depicted together in flight. Rendered in 14K yellow gold, with ruby eyes. The cost? Just $345.00. From Cross Jewelers, 570 Congress Street, Portland, Maine 04101. Call 800-433-2988.

175-177

You know, of course, that green m&ms are aphrodisiacs, don't you?
With that as a start...

- ✝ Present him with a bowl full of them.
- ✝ Carefully open a one-pound bag of m&ms and empty it out. Refill it entirely with green m&ms. Seal it up so it looks like new. Give it to him for a snack.
- ✝ Fill his box of Cheerios with green m&ms.

178

It's romantic—but not that *unusual*—to have tickets to the opera or the Red Sox. Some offbeat romantics have created their own custom "tickets" to the following events and activities:

- ✓ Dinner for two. (Reserved seating only.)
- ✓ Season tickets for "Friday Night Mattress Testing."
- ✓ A personal striptease. (Front row seat.)
- ✓ An evening together. Sans kids. Sans TV. Sans phone. Sans clothes.

179

Prize winner: *Most Memorable Excuse for Not Being Romantic:* "I come from one big, happy, dysfunctional family."

180

Prize winner: *Most Offbeat Comment During a Discussion of Feelings:* "I'm getting in touch with my Inner Klingon."

181

Prize winner: *Best Headline in a Customized Direct Mail Campaign to a Boyfriend:* "Romance Me *Now*—Beat the Valentine's Rush! Details Inside. More Fun Where Prohibited by Law."

182

. . . .

It's possible to go through a lot of life on "Auto Pilot"—getting through, but not really "being there" with your full attention. Those who put their intimate relationship on Auto Pilot find that it *can* work—for a *while*. But eventually your co-pilot will fly the coop.

183

. . . .

Camp out in your backyard.

184

. . . .

There's something wonderfully *indulgent* about romance. We take time. We give of ourselves. We share our emotions. We indulge our fantasies. We indulge each other. (Romance and fear are opposites. Romance and stinginess don't go together. Romance and small-mindedness don't mix.)

185

For you parents who may feel guilty about being romantic, for fear that you're taking time, money or attention away from your kids: You are hereby *absolved!* When you give to your mate, you give to your children. There is no better way to *teach* love than to *practice* love. (You *know* that kids are much better at watching and emulating than they are at *listening!*)

186-188

When dining out...

- ♠ Arrange to have a small gift delivered to your table just before the main course is served.
- ♠ Arrange to have a dozen red roses delivered to your table.
- ♠ Hire a musician to serenade your lover at your table.

You mustn't force sex to do the work of love
or love to do the work of sex.

~ Mary McCarthy

189-191

. . . .

Current romantic favorites in the Godek Music Library:

- ▲ *Shepherd Moons*, by Enya
- ▲ *In the Garden*, by Eric Tingstad & Nancy Rumbel
- ▲ *Reference Point*, by Acoustic Alchemy

192

. . . .

Love will add more years to your life than any diet or exercise program will.

193

. . . .

"The problem with holidays is that we turn them into days that attempt to make up for all the *other* days. This is too much of a burden for one little 24-hour period. This is why we need to create our own personal holidays, private celebrations, and special rituals." {Gail M., Boston}

194

· ·

Here's a new source for long-stemmed chocolate roses: Lyla's Chocolates. Half a dozen for just $25.75; and a dozen for $40 (includes ground shipping). Packed in a rose box, with baby's breath. Important note: Shipping is available only October through May—because the summer heat does more than wilt these tasty roses! Write to 417 Miller Ave, Mill Valley, CA 94941, or call 415-383-8887.

195

· ·

Why do we wear wedding rings on the "ring finger"? Tradition. The ancient Greeks and Romans believed that a nerve ran from that finger directly to the heart.

196

· ·

The longer you're together, the more *subtle* your romantic gestures can be. The better you know one another, the more *meaningful* your romantic gestures can be.

197

Planning to renew your wedding vows in a second ceremony? [You romantic *fools*, you!] These books may help make the occasion extra special:

- ➤ *Weddings for Grownups*, by Carroll Stoner
- ➤ *I Do: A Guide to Creating Your Own Unique Wedding Ceremony*, by Sydney Barbara Metrick
- ➤ *Weddings By Design*, by Richard Leviton

198-200

Songs that received the most votes in my informal survey of American's favorite lovesongs:

- ✳ *I Will Always Love You*, by Whitney Houston
- ✳ *As Time Goes By*, from *Casablanca*
- ✳ *The Wind Beneath My Wings*, by Bette Midler

201

. . . .

The life of a radio DJ is a *hard* one . . . *especially* if you try to be as creative in your *own* romantic gestures as you are in your radio promotions. Take, for example, Kidd Kraddick at KISS-FM in Dallas. He once arranged for a listener to greet his girlfriend as a knight on horseback! He sent *another* couple to sex therapy! (And *then* had them report their progress on the air!)

And here's the birthday celebration he concocted for his wife recently: He took her out for drinks—where they "happened" to run into two of her best friends. They accompanied them to a restaurant—where they "bumped" into a few *more* of her friends. They spent the rest of the evening traveling around town, gathering friends that Kidd had planted in various locations! Way to go, Kidd!

202

. . . .

An artist in New York City is using the "medium" of graffiti to express his love for his wife. So when you see some especially grand renderings of the name "Sally" on some brick wall or water tower, you now know they're "J's" public tokens of love.

203

Have your handwriting analyzed! The art and science of graphology has come a long way, and you'll be amazed at what can be "read" in your writing.

204

And just to show you that we romantics don't always take ourselves too seriously, we recommend *Binky's Guide to Love*, a hilarious (and twisted) cartoon book by Matt Groening (creator of the Simpsons).

205

John Gray—who discovered that *Men Are From Mars, Women Are From Venus*—now reveals *What Your Mother Couldn't Tell You & Your Father Didn't Know (Advanced Relationship Skills for Lasting Intimacy & Great Sex)*. Good books, long titles!

206

A note from the Don't-Put-All-Your-Eggs-In-One-Basket Department:

You need friends! —To pal-around with, to relax with, and to take the pressure off your love relationship. No *one* person can meet *all* your relationship needs. Having friends will help strengthen your love relationship.

207

They tell me that in Hawaii, when a woman wears a flower over her left ear, it means "I'm taken." A flower over her right ear means "I'm available." Perhaps you could create some personal signals for communicating with your partner.

208

One memorable evening in the Romance Class, Cindy W. answered a long-standing question among many men. "Why do women enjoy dancing so much? Why, we thought you knew! *Dancing is foreplay.*"

209-210

- ❦ **News for men:** *Women are not men.*
- ❦ **News for women:** *Men are not women.*

211-212

- ❊ **News for women:** Men are a *little* more subtle than you thought. Yes, we're rather straightforward about sex, but we often like to have a little bit left to the imagination. A little satin and lace has been known to lure a man away from the TV!
- ❊ **News for men:** Women like sex, too! They're simply on a different speed, and they need more attention to environment and foreplay than you do. (You don't take a sports car from zero to 60 without warming-up the engine first, do you?!)

213

Have you ever tried to buy a *heart-shaped box* at any time of the year *other* than Valentine's Day? It's nearly *impossible* to find one! The solution? Stock up on them early in February! Great for wrapping romantic surprises year-round!

214-216

Readers recommend . . . Romantic inns and bed & breakfasts:

- ✦ **Ventana Inn, Big Sur, California:** Enjoy your own hot tub overlooking the Pacific Ocean, then dine in the on-site, four-star restaurant. Call 800-628-6500.
- ✦ **Grant Corner Inn, Santa Fe, New Mexico:** Elegance and comfort. Many rave reviews from readers over the years. Call 505-983-6678.
- ✦ **The Inn at Perry Cabin, St. Michaels, Maryland:** Nineteenth Century ambiance combined with Twentieth Century luxury. Call 800-722-2949.

217

. . . .

You haven't *really* been on a romantic Caribbean vacation until you've experienced one of Sandals Resorts. These folks really, truly know how to create a romantic atmosphere. When they say "Ultra all-inclusive luxury resorts for couples only" they *mean* it! Luxurious accommodations, unbelievable service, no kids, no hassles, no pulling out your wallet every time you turn around. They have several resorts on Jamaica, Antigua, St. Lucia and Barbados. Call Sandals at 888-SANDALS!

218

. . . .

Play miniature golf . . . while dressed in your wedding gown and tuxedo!

219

. . . .

Try this next Saturday evening: Prepare a five-course dinner—and serve each course in a different room of your home. Choose any rooms you wish, but dessert *must* be served in the bedroom. *Bon appétit!*

220

. . . .

I'm often asked by single folks what I think about dating services, personal ads, matchmaking services, etc. My opinion is that they're *all* fine. The *key* is to match your style and your comfort level with the technique. What works for one person won't necessarily work for the next.

Several participants in my Romance Classes have reported glowingly about *Great Expectations*, the world's oldest and largest video introduction service. They say it removes the guesswork, frustration and awkwardness of meeting other singles. The opportunities are many: *Great Expectations* has 50 locations in North America, with 165,000+ members. And the statistics are impressive: They boast an estimated 10,000 marriages! Call 818-788-5200 for the centre nearest you!

221

. . . .

Save some mistletoe from Christmas—and use it in *July!*

222

As you know, Valentine's Day is an "unofficial" holiday. It doesn't merit speeches, parades or even a day off work . . . Just millions of individual, intimate celebrations. [Hmmm . . . Perhaps this is as it *should* be.]

223

How many *minutes per day of **undivided attention*** do you give your lover?

224

Could it be that romantic love is a key to *spiritual growth?* Perhaps in loving another, giving to another, in a deep and intimate way, we connect more directly with our own soul, and touch the source of all Love. (Several philosophers, including Plato, Castellanus and Petrarch, have suggested so.)

225-227

. . . .

"A-to-Z Romantic Exclamations": Write a series of 26 "romantic thoughts" to your partner. Begin each one with a word that starts with a different letter of the alphabet:

Always and forever—that's how long I'll love you!

Be my one-and-only!

Come closer—never leave me!

228-230

. . . .

"A-to-Z Romantic Affirmations": Write a series of 26 paragraphs about different "themes" that begin with all the different letters of the alphabet:

Affection: When I think of you, my affection knows no bounds . . . etc.

Beginnings: Every day with you is a new beginning . . . etc.

Commitment: When I married you, I promised to stand by your side . . . etc.

231-233

. . . .

"A-to-Z Romantic Gifts": I think you *know* what to do!

Artwork, azaleas, Aretha Franklin albums . . . etc.

Balloons, books, Beatles 45s, Baileys Irish Creme . . . etc.

Chocolate, CDs, cookies, cupcakes, candles, cards . . . etc.

234

. . . .

Is your husband highly analytical? Conduct a "scientific study" of which lingerie he prefers. What colors? What styles? What materials? [This "study" could go on for *years!*] Chart your progress. Write a report. Couldn't hurt. Might help!

235

. . . .

At Swedish Autos Inc. in Farmers Branch, Texas, they're offering a free marriage ceremony with every 30,000-mile inspection on Hondas, Volvos and BMWs (!)

236

Sigmund Freud once said: "The great question that has never been answered and which I have not yet been able to answer, despite my thirty years of research into the feminine soul, is: *What does woman want?*" Well, if ol' Sigmund had simply read a Harlequin Romance, he'd know!

237

Don't simply send flowers . . . Make your flowers into a meaningful and symbolic gift. Give some *special thought* to your note: "The white freesia symbolize the light you've brought into my life. The yellow daffodils remind me of the gold in our wedding rings. The red roses symbolize the bloom of our love."

238

The love of your mate is worth more than the fleeting adoration of a hundred strangers.

You give but little when you give your posses-
sions.
It is when you give of yourself that you truly
give.

~ Kahlil Gibran

239-242

Some favorite inscriptions on the inside surface of wedding rings:

- ✧ A.A.F. (Always And Forever)
- ✧ G.M.F.L. (Geese Mate For Life)
- ✧ A.T.S.B.O. (And They Shall Be One.)
- ✧ T.L.Y.T.I.E.T.T.L.Y.M. (Ask a Beatles fan. Hint: From *Abbey Road*.)

243

From the scientific world we now have proof that a *true aphrodisiac* exists, and has been sitting right under our noses for *ages!* It's alcohol. And it only works on women. True! The journal *Nature* reports that alcohol stimulates the production of testosterone in women. Testosterone has been linked to sexual arousal in women. (Ironically, alcohol *depresses* sexual arousal in men. What a cruel, cruel world!)

244

Unique, hand-lettered and hand-painted cards are now available from Crane. Every card is one-of-a-kind. They are truly the most *elegant* greeting cards you've ever seen. The words are rendered in eye-popping calligraphy, with messages such as "Yes!" "Love you." "Happy Anniversary." "Please!" "I miss you." Available only in finer stationery-type stores. Or call direct at 800-IS-CRANE.

245

The all-purpose, do-it-yourself, customizable romantic item! (Fill it in and give it to your lover.)

_____

_____

_____

_____

246

Hug more.

247

Complain less.

248

Give more.

249

Criticize less.

250

Play more.

251

Work less.

252

Listen more.

253

Worry less.

254

. . . .

A couple exercise: Each of you write-down your *personal definition* of these words. You have five minutes per word to ponder and write. Then compare your answers and discuss. (There's no right or wrong here!)

- ❏ Love
- ❏ Couple
- ❏ Compromise
- ❏ Happiness
- ❏ Marriage
- ❏ Responsibility
- ❏ Passion
- ❏ Intimacy
- ❏ Masculine/feminine

255

. . . .

If the two of you seem to *think* differently, perhaps you *do!* Perhaps you're a left-brained (logical/analytical) type, while your partner is a right-brained (creative/intuitive) type. Check-out the new book *When Opposites Attract: Right-Brain/Left-Brain Relationships and How to Make Them Work*, by Rebecca Cutter. The book includes a test to help you determine your "thinking style".

256

Two books you may want to peruse: *Customs and Superstitions and Their Romantic Origins*, by Rudolph Barach. And *Curious Customs*, by Tad Tuleja.

257

Overheard at a recent Mensa meeting: "Just because I'm *smart* doesn't mean I understand *women!*" [Mensa is the international high-IQ society.] {J.M., NYC}

258

Do you and your partner have the same "Vacation Style"? Are you an "Adventurer," "Sight-Seer," "Romantic," "Shopper," "Athlete," or "Indulger"? Do you choose vacation destinations and activities that match your styles? How do you compromise when you have different styles?

259

Currently enjoying a resurgence of interest is the arcane Personality Type System called the Enneagram. It's an ancient system based on a circle with nine points on its perimeter. Nine personality types are revealed and described: 1) The perfectionist, 2) the giver, 3) the performer, 4) the tragic romantic, 5) the observer, 6) the devil's advocate, 7) the epicure, 8) the boss, and 9) the mediator. For more info, see these books: *The Enneagram: Understand Yourself and the Others in Your Life*, by Helen Palmer; and *Enneagram Transformations*, by Don Richard Riso.

260

The four basic *romantic* food groups:

- ☞ Aphrodisiacs
- ☞ Wine
- ☞ Chocolate
- ☞ Pizza

261

Give your lover a series of boxes—elegant metal boxes, fancy cardboard boxes, etc. Place inside each box a small slip of paper with one word written in calligraphy: "Devotion." "Love." "Adoration." "Passion." "Support." etc.

262

One couple in the Romance Class explained that they've created a ritual for ridding themselves of negativity, thus making more room for love. Twice a year they buy a bunch of helium balloons. They label each balloon with a marker: "Anger." "Jealousy." "Fear." "Guilt." "Impatience." They then take all of these balloons outside and symbolically release their negative feelings and problems. Cool, huh?!

263

Create a comic strip based on the two of you, your friends and families!

264

Change *one little thing* about your normal daily routine—something that adds a little *spice*, a little *excitement* to your life.

265

Change one little thing about how you *talk* with your partner today.

266

Change one little thing about your normal routine of *lovemaking*.

267

Roll out the red carpet—*literally!*—for your lover! Find a red rug, maybe *rent* one! Roll it out your front door and down the stairs. Treat him like royalty. Make her your Queen-For-A-Day!

268-269

▲ *Best* romantic gift for women: *Jewelry*
▲ *Worst* romantic gift for women: *An exercise video*

270-271

♠ *Best* romantic gift for men: *Anything electronic*
♠ *Worst* romantic gift for men: *Socks*

272-273

🍃 *Best* romantic gesture for women: *Breakfast in bed*
🍃 *Worst* romantic gesture for women: *Cooking a great meal—but not cleaning-up!*

274-275

✓ *Best* romantic gesture for men: *Anything sexual*
✓ *Worst* romantic gesture for men: *Taking him to a ballgame—but complaining*

276

. . . .

Love is like a ripple in a pond. *You* are in the center. Once you love *yourself,* you can then send ripples of love out to those closest to you—your mate, your family. Your love then ripples outward to friends, neighbors and relatives. And finally, it can ripple out to strangers and the world as a whole. You can't "love" mankind if you don't first love *yourself.*

277

. . . .

When daily life gets to be "too much"—when you're *frazzled* . . . What's your favorite escape? Where's your favorite hideout? What's your favorite leisure activity? Do you know your *partner's* answers to these questions? The answers should spark some romantic ideas. If they *don't,* either you're brain-dead, or your partner is *really* boring.

278

You're familiar with the concept of the "Inner Child," right? Well, perhaps we all have inside of us an "Inner Romantic." —He/she is that *expressive, exuberant* part of us; the *passionate, creative and giving* side of our personality.

279

According to philosopher/psychologist William James, happiness is reflected in the ratio of one's accomplishments to one's aspirations. What are your romantic accomplishments? Your relationship aspirations?

280

Planning a little romantic trip? Fly on *Tuesdays, Wednesdays* and *Saturdays* to get the lowest airfares. Fewer people fly on these days, so the airlines usually lower their prices to fill seats. (Friday afternoons and Monday mornings are the *busiest* times.)

281

. . . .

Don't take life too seriously. Don't take *yourself* too seriously, either. But you *must* take your partner and your relationship seriously!

282

. . . .

Romantics are cheerleaders.
Romantics are the biggest fan of their lovers. They provide enthusiastic support, constant encouragement, and unconditional love. (They don't succeed 100 percent of the time, naturally, but they're always in there trying.)

- ❏ Have you complimented her lately?
- ❏ Have you thanked him recently?

283

. . . .

Go above and beyond. Do the *unexpected.* Give more than you *have to.*

284

. . . .

"Reasons *Not* To Have An Affair—#99": The incidence of death during intercourse comprises less than 1% of sudden coronary deaths. And of *these*, 70% occur during extramarital relations. Experts guess that guilt and anxiety are linked to the heart attacks, not the sex itself. {From *Love & Sex After Sixty*, by Dr. Robert Butler & Myrna Lewis.}

285

. . . .

Decide to fall in love all over again. That's it—just *decide.* You don't need to read books that analyze your relationship. You don't need therapy. You just need to *decide.* Just think of the great opportunity you have: The less romantic you've been, the more dramatic the change will be! I've had guys in the Romance Class simply *make up their minds* to be more romantic. They've reported that this simple decision led to their falling in love with their wives all over again. (Who am I to argue with success?)

Love is not a matter of counting the years—
but making the years count.

~ Michelle St. Amand

286

Loads o' fun and lots of cool gift ideas . . . at the Warner Brothers stores. Not *just* for people who are in touch with their "Inner Child"—but also for those in touch with their "Inner Bugs Bunny" and "Inner Superman"! They've got 54 stores across the U.S.! Visit or call 800-223-6524.

287

Romance is not about making grand, extraordinary gestures. It is about seeing and appreciating the extraordinary in the everyday and ordinary.

288

Have you ever wondered why the details of Adam and Eve's life together in the Garden of Eden are missing from the *Bible?* A wonderful and creative book, *The Lost Book of Paradise*, brings the first human couple alive for us. Author David Rosenberg weaves a story of mythic proportions: The ultimate romance of Adam and Eve.

289

. . . .

A deep, inspiring and thought-provoking book: *The Art of Intimacy*, by Thomas Patrick Malone & Patrick Thomas Malone.

290

. . . .

Which of these statements best describes you or your beliefs?

1. *Love is a goal worth achieving*
2. *Heart, mind and spirit*
3. *Actions speak louder than words*
4. *Inspiring idealists*
5. *Relationships should never be boring*
6. *You can never be too close*
7. *Lean on me*
8. *The relationship is everything*
9. *Service before self*
10. *Any relationship can be improved*
11. *Can this person truly be this unassuming?*
12. *In love, it's the mind that matters*
13. *Love is making the most of each moment*
14. *Relationships are just another challenge*
15. *Stand by your lover*
16. *Good relationships require leadership*

These 16 personality types are detailed in *16 Ways To Love Your Lover*, by Otto Kroeger & Janet Thuesen.

291

. . . .

"It is impossible to offer anyone *constructive criticism. Constructive* means to build up and *criticism* means to tear down. It is impossible to do both at the same time." Larry Winget, in *Stuff That Works Every Single Day.*

292

. . . .

Give your time freely and gladly to *those* you love and to *causes* you love. Guard your time *jealously,* and give it *carefully,* to everyone and everything else.

293

. . . .

Romance for the musically inclined: Write-out a few bars of the musical score of a lovesong. Send it to your partner without a title and without the words. The challenge is for him or her to figure-out what song it is. {Thanks to Ray and Diane M., of Woodland Hills, California}

294

Monday: Write a quick note to your partner before you leave for work this morning—Start it with, "Three reasons I love you . . ."

295

Tuesday: Write a quick note to your partner before you leave for work this morning—Start it with, "Three things you do that bring a smile to my face . . ."

296

Wednesday's note: "Three things I'm going to change, because you want me to . . ."

297

Thursday's note: "Three ideas for romantic get-aways during the next year . . ."

298

Friday's note: "Three things I'm going to do this weekend to show you how much I love you . . ."

299

Share.

300

Care.

301

Dare.

302

The rich, the famous, and the "great" are rarely good role models for loving relationships. The divorce rate among Hollywood stars is something like 99%, isn't it? The unhappiness of millionaires is legendary. And the infidelities of history's "great" are evidence of deep-seated insecurities. Makes you glad to be *you*, doesn't it?!

303

"bang ghajnIS tlhingan pu' je." *Translated, means* **"Klingons need love, too!"**

304

Why be romantic? Well, you just may *live longer!* Medical research shows that married people have *lower death rates* than those who are single, widowed or divorced. The mortality rate for single men is *twice* that of married men; the rate for single *women* is 1.5 times that of married women. Draw your *own* conclusions!

305

What is it that makes you *unique* in all the world? —Use it to express your love! What is your *partner's* uniqueness? —Cherish and celebrate it!

306

We all tend to take-on the persona and characteristics of our work/career/profession. If we're not careful, this can harm our intimate relationships by infecting our attitudes and actions with stereotypical, pre-programmed responses. For example, successful lawyers are logical and analytical. This is fine, but it's not appropriate for you to bring these exaggerated tendencies home with you and put your spouse "on trial" during discussions. Successful businesspeople are competitive at work. This is fine, but it's *cooperation*—not *competition*—that will make you successful at *home*.

How do you and your partner bring your work personas home with you? Some people consciously "change gears" for half an hour after returning home. You can, too.

307

Do you *like* your partner? Are you *friends* as well as *lovers?* Imagine that you are simply your partner's best friend . . . What kinds of things would the two of you *do* together—and *for* each other—in the next month?

308

Your lover need not be your *best* friend. But he or she *must* be one of your favorite people in all the world.

309

You don't need to *instantly* and *dramatically* become romantic. (Your partner may think you've suddenly gone insane!) Instead, try this strategy: Make the change *slowly* . . . one day at a time . . . one gesture at a time. You can be a *little* more romantic, can't you?!

310

The following advice is so basic and commonsense that I purposely did not include it in my first three books. But several elderly and wise couples have shared the same bit of advice with my recent Romance Classes . . . so I figured that it was worth repeating: "Treat your spouse with the same respect and courtesy that you extend to friends and acquaintances." Sometimes it's best to return to the simple bits of wisdom that we often overlook.

311

From a survey of readers of *Self Magazine:* "What's the strongest influence on what a person finds romantic?" 57% said movies or TV; 33% said "other"; 29% said parents' relationship; 15% said novels; and 7% said advertisements. What can we conclude from this? First, we'd better stop watching TV! And second, we'd better find out what comprises "other"!

312-314

Where to meet single men:

- ✦ At your health club—skip the aerobic classes and check-out the weight room.
- ✦ Eat out often—and don't bury your nose in a book!
- ✦ Head for your neighborhood home-improvement store.

315-317

Where to meet single women:

- ✧ Do your laundry at the local laundromat (*even* if you own a washer and dryer!)
- ✧ Attend some aerobic classes!
- ✧ Attend singles events. Decent guys are highly prized—*especially* if you dance well!

318

I've recently discovered a wine company that *really* takes romance seriously. The folks at Blossom Hill produce a range of delicious *and* reasonably priced wines—from Chardonnay to Merlot. They're available wherever fine wine is sold, from well-stocked supermarkets to liquor stores. Blossom Hill understands that the *presentation* is just as important as the *product* (or gift). Thus, each bottle has a pretty label featuring flowers in pinks and purples . . . a nice touch of class that will add to the atmosphere of your romantic encounter. So not only does it *taste* good, but it *looks* good, too!

319

Do you *trust* your partner—**completely?** If so, celebrate! If *not*, find out *why* not—and *do* something about it. Trust is an essential cornerstone of all intimate relationships.

320-331

For each month of the year define a "theme" or "topic" to focus-on as a couple.
For example:

- ☞ **January:** *Renewal*
- ☞ **February:** *Playing*
- ☞ **March:** *Sensuality*
- ☞ **April:** *Communication*
- ☞ **May:** *Learning*
- ☞ **June:** *Intimacy*

- ☞ **July:** *Commitment*
- ☞ **August:** *Celebrating*
- ☞ **September:** *Self-esteem*
- ☞ **October:** *Change*
- ☞ **November:** *Forgiveness*
- ☞ **December:** *Appreciation*

332-334

Spin-off ideas from the idea above:

- ❏ Define themes for each day of the week. You'll cycle through the list 52 times in a year, giving you variety *and* repetition.
- ❏ Define themes for your *weekends.*
- ❏ One couple in the Romance Class is compiling a list of 365 themes, one for each day of the week. [Some romantics are *obsessed!*]

335

* Chances that an American wedding will occur in June: 1 in 9
* Tons of gold made into wedding rings each year in the United States: 17
* Percentage of American men who say they would marry the same woman if they had it to do all over again: 80
* Percentage of women who say they would marry the same man: 50

{From *The Complete Harper's Index*}

336

Mind-Shifting Exercise #1: Stop "working" on your relationship—and start "playing" with your relationship.

337

Celebrate without reason. Give without strings. Love without stopping. Feel without fear. Dance without music.

338

Mind-Shifting Exercise #99: What if . . . your eyes crossed every time you complained? What if . . . you gave the absolute best of yourself to your partner? What if . . . the person next to you could hear your thoughts? From a great little book, *What If?* by Susan Le Page Simmons. It presents "310 bite-size brain snacks to spark your creative spirit." Available in bookstores or online.

339

Mind-Shifting Exercise #100: Fill-in the blanks:

- ❤ *What if . . .* I followed my heart and _____
- ❤ *What if . . .* I expressed more _____
- ❤ *What if . . .* I changed the way I _____

Everything that touches us, me and you,
takes us together like a violin's bow,
which draws one voice out of two separate things.

~ Rainer Maria Rilke

340-346

. . . .

- ☞ Romance is the process . . . Love is the goal.
- ☞ Romance is a *state of mind.* It's not so much *what* you do, as *how* you do it.
- ☞ Romance is a *state of being.* It's about taking *action* on your feelings.
- ☞ Romance is the language of love.
- ☞ Romance is *Adult Play.*
- ☞ Romance is the environment in which love flourishes.
- ☞ Romance is a *process*—it's not an *event.*

347

. . . .

Create a custom music tape of romantic instrumental music—background music.
This kind of music is great for creating the right environment for candlelit
dinners or romantic lovemaking sessions.

348

For fans of the romantic movie favorite, *Somewhere In Time*, the Grand Hotel holds an annual "Somewhere In Time Festival"! Fans, cast and crew members gather toward the end of October every year for a weekend of lectures, panel discussions, trivia contests, and, of course, elegant receptions and cocktail parties. The cost? Just $869 per couple. Call the Grand Hotel on Mackinac Island in Michigan at: 800-33-GRAND.

349

If your lover is a Superman fan (and there are *lots* of them out there!), head for the annual "Superman Celebration" in—where else?!—*Metropolis*, Illinois. Visit the Super Museum; pose next to the giant Superman statue; participate in the country-fair-style activities, including costume contests and arm wrestling competitions! Held early in June, the Superman Celebration is co-sponsored by the local newspaper (*The Metropolis Planet*) and the Metropolis Chamber of Commerce. Call for more info: 800-949-5740.

350-352

. . . .

Understanding your "personality type" can help you communicate and get along with your partner. There are a variety of systems available, some of which are explored in these books:

- ❖ *Who Do You Think You Are?* by Keith Harary & Eileen Donahue
- ❖ *How Can I Get Through To You?—Breakthrough Communication,* by D. Glenn Foster & Mary Marshall
- ❖ An easy and fun "typing" system called the PACE Palette is also available from the PACE Organization. A kit of color-coded personality descriptions is just $6.95. Write to PACE, Box 1378, Studio City, California 91614, or call 818-769-5100.

353

. . . .

How and when did you realize you'd become a "couple"?

354

How did kissing originate? Glad you asked. Some people believe that kissing evolved from ancient humans touching faces and smelling one another. Others conjecture that the kiss developed because primitive humans believed that breath contained a portion of our deepest essence, and that by kissing each other we mingle our souls. (And you thought "a kiss was just a kiss"!)

355

We have "kissing," "smooching," and "sucking face." But the ancient Romans were a little more specific. A kiss between acquaintances was called a "basium." A kiss between close friends was an "osculum." And a kiss between lovers was a "suavium."

356

You've seen the bumper sticker "Think globally. Act locally"? How about "Love everyone. Practice on your partner"?!

357
. . . .

I've been joking about some guys being "Romantically Impaired" for several years. Jenny P., of Miami, used this concept as a springboard to have a little fun with her "impaired-but-teachable" husband Jim. She created a "romantically impaired" symbol: A heart inside a circle with a diagonal slash through it (like a no-smoking sign). She drew it on the bathroom mirror with soap. She had a bumper sticker made for his car. She drew on their driveway in chalk: "Parking for the Romantically Impaired."

Yes, Jim has become more romantic. But he has also returned the favor: He had a doctor friend diagnose Jenny as being "Incurably and Contagiously Romantic." In the works are a variety of cures, including jellybean pills and prescriptions for vacations.

358
. . . .

"Quality of life" is not about the quality of your *stuff*—VW vs. BMW—but about the quality of your *relationships*.

359-361

· ·

Ideas courtesy of my friends at Xerox:

- ‣ Get a photo of your honey blown-up to poster size.
- ‣ Make lots of copies of favorite photos of the two of you. Wallpaper a room with the copies.
- ‣ Create a life-size cardboard stand-up of yourself to give to your partner!

362

· ·

For your *Star Trek* fan: The Official Star Fleet Academy Ring! Available in 10K or 14K gold, these rings—in men's and women's styles—are made by Jostens (the college ring folks) and were commissioned by the official Star Trek Fan Club. Rings are available at Viacom in Chicago. Call 312-867-3500.

363

Accept the fact that one partner will be more romantic than the other. That's just the way it *is*, folks! The goal is *not* to become equal/identical—it is, rather, to encourage and allow each partner to express his or her love in their own, individual, unique way.

364

A *must* for your Romantic Resource Library: *How To Really Love The One You're With,* by Larry James. This book is revealing and empowering. It provides many insights that will assist you in achieving a healthy love relationship anchored in unconditional love. Available in bookstores or by calling 800-725-9223.

365

How do you measure your life? In income—or intimacy? In inches and pounds—or kisses and hugs? In status symbols—or symbols of love?

366-367

. . . .

Romantic ways to use your lover's pager/beeper:

☆ Call the pager number, then punch 0-1-1-3-4. It spells "HELLO."

☆ Call the pager number, then punch 1-4-3. It stands for "I LOVE YOU."

368

. . . .

The most-often-asked question in my Romance Class is: "How can I get my partner to *change?*" The answer is: *You* change! Change the way you *treat* him or her. Change the way you *think about* him or her. Change some habits, some routines, some expectations. —And you'll discover your partner changing. You see, *you're* the only one you really have any control over. You can't change another person. You can only create a climate that is safe for change; that is supportive of change; that is patient with the time it will take to change.

369

....

Days to celebrate—for music lovers:

- ♥ February 26: Johnny Cash's birthday
- ♥ March 25: Elton John's birthday
- ♥ May 1: Judy Collins' birthday
- ♥ July 26: Mick Jagger's birthday
- ♥ September 23: Bruce Springsteen's birthday
- ♥ October 14: Justin Hayward's birthday
- ♥ December 1: Bette Midler's birthday

370

....

Days to celebrate—for sports fans:

- ♥ April 16: Kareem Abdul-Jabbar's birthday
- ♥ June 11: Joe Montana's birthday
- ♥ August 4: Roger Clemens' birthday
- ♥ October 20: Mickey Mantle's birthday

371

Days to celebrate—for hopeless romantics:

- ❦ March 12: James Taylor's birthday
- ❦ March 31: Leo Buscaglia's birthday
- ❦ June 18: Paul McCartney's birthday
- ❦ November 26 (1942): The film *Casablanca* premiered at Hollywood Theater in New York

372

Days to celebrate—for humor lovers:

- ❧ March 14: Billy Crystal's birthday
- ❧ April 26: Carol Burnett's birthday
- ❧ June 28: Mel Brooks' birthday
- ❧ July 28: "Garfield" creator Jim Davis' birthday
- ❧ November 22: Rodney Dangerfield's birthday
- ❧ November 26: "Peanuts" creator Charles M. Schulz's birthday

373

. . . .

Days to celebrate—for late-nite TV fans:

- ✸ April 12: David Letterman's birthday
- ✸ April 28: Jay Leno's birthday
- ✸ October 23: Johnny Carson's birthday

374

. . . .

Days to celebrate—for movie buffs:

- ✴ March 19: Glenn Close's birthday
- ✴ March 31: Shirley Jones' birthday
- ✴ May 20: Cher's birthday
- ✴ June 22: Meryl Streep's birthday
- ✴ July 30: Arnold Schwarzenegger's birthday
- ✴ August 8: Dustin Hoffman's birthday
- ✴ October 4: Charlton Heston's birthday

375

. . . .

You say you just don't have *time* to be romantic? The #1 time-stealer is *television*. Try this experiment: *Stop watching TV for one solid month.* I'll bet your time shortage will *evaporate*.

376

. . . .

Celebrate "Valentine's Day" on the 14th of every month—*except* February!

377

. . . .

Create a "Couples Time Capsule" and bury it in your backyard. Make a map so you can find the capsule in 20 years. Items to include: Personal keepsakes; photos of the two of you; current newspapers and magazines. Write letters to your partner that he or she won't see for 20 years! Describe your life and love today; express your hopes, dreams and aspirations for the future.

378-379

. . . .

Some engaging ideas from Romance Class participants:
- ➤ Romantic hiding places for diamond rings: Inside boxes of Cracker Jacks (what a prize!), among flowers, at the bottom of champagne glasses, tied to balloons.
- ➤ Romantic locations for proposals—Don't forget that *your* definition of what's romantic doesn't necessarily apply to everyone!: Baseball stands, classy restaurants, fast food restaurants, in bed, in elevators, in the place where you first met, in subway cars, over the phone, on cassette tape, at the beach, on vacation…

380

. . . .

Love is easy when it's easy. It's the *hard times* that will reveal the depth of your love, and the strength of your commitment.

Regardless of the question, love is the answer.

~ Anonymous

381

Readers' favorites from *1001 Ways To Be Romantic:*

- ❤ Buy gifts ahead-of time, and warehouse them in a "Gift Closet."
- ❤ You know, of course, that green **m**&**m**'s are aphrodisiacs, don't you?!
- ❤ Use "Love Stamps" when you mail those love letters and cards!
- ❤ Write "I LOVE YOU" on the bathroom mirror with a piece of soap.
- ❤ Create a "Romantic Idea Jar": Write 100 romantic ideas on separate slips of paper. Fill a jar with them. Once a week, each of you can pick an idea.
- ❤ Create custom fortunes for Chinese Fortune Cookies.
- ❤ Place a flower under the windshield wiper of her car.
- ❤ Place a flower in his briefcase.
- ❤ Tape your photo to your pillow when you leave on a business trip.
- ❤ Eat dinner by candlelight. Heck—eat *breakfast* by candlelight!
- ❤ Fake a power outage at home. Bring out the candles!

382

. . . .

Readers' favorites from *1001 **More** Ways To Be Romantic:*

- ✦ Get re-married (to the same person) every year! You'll be a newlywed forever!
- ✦ Issue a "Romance Report Card." Grade him or her from **A+** to **F** in these categories: Intimacy, Creativity, Gifts, Communication, Thoughtfulness.
- ✦ Wrap yourself up and wait for your lover underneath the Christmas tree!
- ✦ *Choose well.* Choosing a compatible partner is perhaps the most overlooked ingredient in creating a romantic relationship.
- ✦ Create a "5-Sense Evening," during which you and your lover stimulate *all five* of each other's senses!
- ✦ Canopy beds.
- ✦ Edible flowers (!)—Tiger lilies, zucchini flowers, nasturtiums, rose geraniums.
- ✦ Visit Love, Arizona; Bliss, New York; Valentine, Montana; or Romeo, Florida.
- ✦ Call 800-528-STAR, to buy a star for your lover!
- ✦ Call 800-LOVEBOAT to book a romantic cruise with Princess Cruises.

383

· ·

Readers' favorites from *Romance 101:*

- ☆ Be yourself. Be unique. Be *eccentric.* —It's what's most lovable about you!

- ☆ Remember that a relationship is a *celebration* as well as a responsibility.

- ☆ Discuss with your partner:
    - ❏ What's the difference between *affection* and *courtesy?*
    - ❏ What's the difference between *having sex* and *making love?*
    - ❏ What's the difference between *talking* and *communicating?*

- ☆ Love is a *habit!* Practice these good habits:
    - ➤ Focus on your good memories instead of the bad.
    - ➤ Show appreciation more often.
    - ➤ Begin your day by telling your partner one specific thing you love about him or her.

- ☆ Learn the "Vacuum Kiss": While kissing, you suck the air out of each other's mouths, and then you separate with a *Pop!*

384

. . . .

Favorites from *The Lovers' Bedside Companion:*

- ☞ "Love doesn't teach, it shows the way. Love doesn't lecture, it just loves!"
- ☞ "Commitment requires daily renewal."
- ☞ "Gifts are symbols. They represent you when you're not physically there."
- ☞ "You can only be *truly known* in an intimate, long-term relationship."
- ☞ "The wedding merely affirms the marriage."
- ☞ "Celebrate *something* every month."
- ☞ "Lovers listen with their hearts."
- ☞ "Love does not—*cannot*—hurt. It's the *absence* of love that hurts."
- ☞ "Become an artist of your relationship."
- ☞ "Passive people never live passionate lives."
- ☞ "Relationships aren't 50/50—they're 100/100."
- ☞ "The history of humankind is the story of our search for love."

385

↔ Does she love ice cream as much as she loves you? Take her on a tour of Ben & Jerry's factory in Waterbury, Vermont! Call 802-244-TOUR.

↔ Does he crave beer as much as he craves you? Take him to the world's largest brewery, Anheuser-Busch, in St. Louis, Missouri. Call 314-577-2626.

↔ Is she a certified chocoholic? Take her to Hershey's Chocolate World, in Hershey, Pennsylvania. Call 717-534-4900.

386

Did you know that there are *two* kinds of romantic restaurants?

♥ The elegant/active/often-with-great-views restaurant
♥ The small/dark/cozy-with-tiny-tables restaurant

Which kind of restaurant does she prefer? Don't take her to *one* when she's crazy about the *other*.

387

. . . .

And then there was the "Conversation Candy Heart" that wouldn't die. Back on Valentine's Day 1981, Hank S. took one of those little candy hearts with "LUV U" printed on it, and placed it on his wife's pillow. Toni saved it until their anniversary in July, when she hid it inside one of his socks. Thus began a tradition of trading this little candy keepsake back-and-forth for over a *decade*. (They recently reported that they've had it encased in *Plexiglas*, because it was gettting a bit worn-out!)

388

. . . .

From the "Spare No Expense" File: If you've got $4.5 million that you're not sure what to do with, you *could* buy your honey a personal luxury submarine! The 65-foot, NOMAD 1000 is made by U.S. Submarines of Anacortes, Washington. The thing can dive to 1,000 feet and remain underwater for 10 days. Amenities include plush seats, walnut tables, hot showers and "a toilet with an incredible view!" according to company president Bruce Jones.

389

For the truly committed chocolate lover: *Chocolatier Magazine!* According to the editors, this bi-monthly magazine is "for those whose passion for life is exemplified by their love for chocolate." Write to *Chocolatier*, 45 West 34th Street, Suite 600, New York City, New York 10001, or call 212-239-0855. {Special thanks to Elisa Fershtadt!}

390

What are your talents—your special gifts? Do you use them to express your love?

391

And then, of course, there's the *I Love Chocolate! Cookbook*, by Mrs. Fields! Included are 100 all-new, incredibly decadent recipes from the woman who single-handedly reinvented the chocolate chip cookie.

The day will come when,
after harnessing the ether, the winds,
the tides, gravitation, we shall harness for God
the energies of love.
And, on that day, for the second time in the
history of the world, man will have
discovered fire.

~ Pierre Teilhard de Chardin

392

. . . .

After 20 years of marriage, during which they had eight children in 11 years, Helen and Joe Hesketh found their marriage falling apart. One night, Helen sat down with a pad of paper and, fighting back tears, picked up a pen and wrote a love letter to Joe. The next day he wrote back. Then she wrote again. And he answered again. This began an incredible correspondence that has spanned the last *20 years* and has resulted in *14,600 love letters!* Today, at 61 years of age, the Hesketh's are deeply and passionately in love; they give inspirational talks nationwide; and—need you ask?— they continue to write love letters every day!

393

. . . .

Yea for our side! According to a Roper poll, reported in *Fortune Magazine*, nearly 80% of respondents defined success as *having a happy family life or relationship.* The *last* of seven choices were money, career and power. *Could this be the beginning of a trend?*

394

How do you form the "habit" of romance? You try. And then you try again, and again and again and *again*. Researchers have shown that people who change habits make an average of *five* attempts before they succeed.

395

Compose a love poem *together*. You write one verse, she writes the next. Work on it for an hour . . . or over the course of a week . . . a month . . . a year . . . a *lifetime!*

396

Ladies: Mail some of your lingerie to him—at *work*. Send him one piece of a two-piece outfit, along with an enticing love note! (Make sure you wrap it well, and include a note on the outside of the package that says, "Be *alone* when you open this envelope." You want to surprise him, not embarrass him!)

397

Begin each day with the words, "I love you," whispered to your lover, while you're still in bed. It will set the tone for your entire day.

398

End each day with the words, "Thank you," whispered to your lover, before you drift off to sleep. It will help bring you peace.

399

Caress with your words. Listen with your heart. Kiss with your eyes.

400

Choose your favorite idea from this book, and *add your own creative twist to it.* Goal: Generate three *new* romantic ideas.

401

Real love stories don't have endings.

About the Author

Gregory Godek is an author and researcher, speaker and performer, husband and father. He is the author of three bestselling books based on his twenty years of teaching Romance Seminars. Greg has appeared on the *Oprah Winfrey Show* conducting a "Mini-Romance Class" and has been featured on *The Donohue Show* discussing "Is Your Lover Among the Romantically Impaired?"

Greg speaks nationally and internationally, presenting keynote speeches and seminars on love and relationships. His books *1001 Ways To Be Romantic* and *10,000 Ways to Say I Love You* are idea books, presenting numbered listings of creative ideas, tips, and resources. His *Love Coupons* is a set of nifty coupons to put those ideas into instant action. Greg now has over one million books in print.

A companion to *this* book is being published simultaneously. Whereas *Romantic Essentials* is a *practical* book, *The Lover's Companion* is an *inspirational* book, which presents the collected wit and wisdom from Greg's Romance Seminars. Together they cover both sides of the "Romantic Equation": The thoughtful, feeling side, and the expressive, action-oriented side.

1001 Ways To Be Romantic

Love Coupon

When signed by the presenter, this coupon
is a contract promising that the items checked will be
the focus of genuine and heartfelt attention during the next week:

    ❐ Trust   ❐ Commitment

    ❐ Intimacy   ❐ Listening

    ❐ Sensuality ❐ Talking

A gift to _____

A gift from _____

1001 Ways To Be Romantic
Love Coupon

This is an Official "I'll Do It *Your* Way" Coupon.

Void where prohibited by law. You must be 18 years or older
in order to participate.

Description of activity: _____

_____

_____

A gift to _____
A gift from _____

Romantic Things to Do Today

_____
_____
_____

Romantic Plans for Next Week

_____
_____
_____

Romantic Plans for Next Month

_____
_____
_____

Romantic Plans for Next Year

_____
_____
_____

Lessons to Review

_____
_____
_____

Personal Affirmations

_____
_____
_____

Romantic Shopping List

_____
_____
_____

Misc. Romantic Ideas

_____
_____
_____

Author's Note

Thank you for investing your time, your resources, your *self*, in enhancing your capacity to love. I believe that there is *nothing* you can do in your *entire life* that will pay back more dividends than **learning to love.**

For those of you who are new to these books—*welcome!* Please join us on the Journey. I sometimes play the *guide*, but more often I'm a fellow traveller. Let's explore together.

For those of you who are old friends—*welcome back!* How've you been?

Here we go again!

Namaste,

~ G.J.P.G.

An Invitation

These books and seminars are part of the Grand Conversation, as Greg calls it. He sees his books as "The beginning of a *dialogue*, and not merely another long-winded monologue by some so-called 'expert'." We would like to hear from *you*.

You are invited to write to us with your romantic ideas and your romantic stories—whether sentimental, outrageous or creative. They may end up in a future book. We will credit you by name or protect your anonymity, as you wish. —Or just write to say *Hi!*

Romantic Ideas
Casablanca Press
Post Office Box 4410
Naperville, IL
60567

1001 Ways To Be Romantic
Love Coupon

This is your basic, all-purpose, customizable and personalizable, do-it-yourself romantic coupon.

_____
_____
_____
_____

A gift to _____
A gift from _____

1001 Ways To Be Romantic

Love Coupon

This coupon entitles you to attend
an event of your choice that requires tickets or reservations.
Here's the deal: The coupon holder gets to choose the
event (value up to $_____).
The coupon issuer gets to pay for the event, and
escort you.

A gift to _____

A gift from _____